MONSTERS

MEDUSA

MONSTERS

MEDUSA

BY Don Nardo
AND Bradley Steffens

KIDHAVEN PRESS

An imprint of Thomson Gale, a part of The Thomson Corporation

THOMSON
★
GALE

Detroit • New York • San Francisco • San Diego • New Haven, Conn.
Waterville, Maine • London • Munich

292.13
NAR

THOMSON
───★───
GALE
™

For Virginia

For more information, contact
KidHaven Press
27500 Drake Rd.
Farmington Hills, MI 48331-3535
Or you can visit our Internet site at http://www.gale.com

LIBRARY OF CONGRESS CATALOGING-IN-PUBLICATION DATA

Nardo, Don, 1947-
Medusa / by Don Nardo and Bradley Steffens.
    p. cm. — (Monsters)
Includes bibliographical references and index.
ISBN 0-7377-2617-2 (hard cover : alk. paper)
1. Medusa (Greek mythology) I. Title. II. Monsters series (KidHaven Press)
BL820.M38N37 2004
398.2'0938'01—dc22
                                          2004011288

Contents

CHAPTER 1

ORIGINS OF THE HIDEOUS SISTERS

The people of ancient Greece believed monsters of all kinds lived in their world. Among the most dangerous of these creatures were the Gorgons, three sisters whose physical appearance was strange and frightening. The most famous of the three was Medusa. According to ancient writers her features were so terrible that any person or other living thing who looked at her turned to stone. Eventually a human hero named Perseus managed to slay Medusa.

Frightening Physical Features

The details of the Gorgons' horrifying appearance vary. One sculpture, found on the island of Corfu, off

Italian artist Caravaggio painted this version of Medusa's hideous head in the 1590s.

the western coast of Greece, portrays a Gorgon with a squat body; a round face with a wide, distorted grin; and bulging eyes. Around her waist the Gorgon wears a belt made of snakes. Some artists depicted Gorgons with snub noses, beards, huge teeth or tusks, and long tongues hanging down onto their chins. Other artists gave them wings, scales, and birdlike claws.

In this nineteenth-century drawing, Gorgons with wings attack a group of humans running for safety.

By far the most unusual and terrifying feature of the Gorgons was their hair. Nests of wriggling snakes covered their heads. One of the earliest writers to mention the hideous sisters was the Athenian playwright Aeschylus. In his play *Prometheus Bound*, written about 460 B.C., he called Medusa and her sisters "the snake-haired Gorgons, whom no man can see and live."[1] About four centuries later the Roman poet and storyteller Ovid described Medusa's "twisting serpents of green hair."[2]

How the Sisters Became Monsters

In his book *Theogony*, written around 700 B.C., the Greek poet Hesiod wrote that the Gorgons were the monstrous offspring of two sea gods, Phorcys and Ceto. Although brother and sister, Phorcys and Ceto married and had six children. Three of the children were old hags who shared a single eye and a single tooth. These hags were known as the Graiae. The other three children were the Gorgons: Medusa, Stheno, and Euryale.

Hesiod said that the Gorgons lived "beyond the stream of the famous Ocean, on the edge [of the world] near night."[3] The "Ocean" Hesiod spoke of was a great waterway that he and other ancient Greeks believed surrounded the land portion of the world. The Gorgons were usually depicted as living on a remote island lying somewhere in the uncharted outer sea.

The ancient Greeks had many stories about how the Gorgons came to be so hideous. Some storytellers said the Gorgons were born ugly. Others said they were made that way as a punishment. According to the most popular legend, the three Gorgons started out as beautiful young women who served as priestesses in one of Athena's temples. Athena was the sister of Zeus, leader of the gods. She also was the goddess of wisdom and war, and she could be very stern and forceful when angry. According to the story, Medusa provoked Athena's wrath by making love to her brother, Poseidon, god of the seas, behind the goddess's back. Even worse, the act took place inside Athena's sacred temple.

When Athena found out about the unholy union, she decided to punish Medusa and her sisters. To ensure that they would always be alone, Athena turned them into monsters. So hideous were the sisters that whoever or whatever saw them would turn to stone. Even plants exposed to the Gorgons hardened to rock.

Magic Powers of the Gorgons

The sight of the Gorgons was deadly, but that was not the only threat they posed. Even small parts of their bodies could be **lethal**. According to one story a single lock of Medusa's hair could turn a person who looked at it to stone. To help the citizens of the Greek city of Tegea ward off attacks, the hero Heracles (whom the Romans called Hercules) brought them a lock of Medusa's hair. He knew

that no one would approach the city while the lock of hair remained at the city gate. He could not get close enough to Medusa to acquire it himself, of course, so he asked for the help of the goddess Athena. Since Athena was immune to the Gorgons' ill effects, she got the hair for Heracles.

According to another tale, Medusa's blood had the power of life and death. A single drop from a vein on one side of Medusa's body was enough to kill a person instantly. However blood from a vein on the opposite side of her body could restore life. Asclepius, a healer who was also the son of the god Apollo, obtained some of Medusa's life-giving

The hero Perseus uses Medusa's head to defeat an enemy in this modern painting.

blood and used it to bring a dead person back to life. This angered Zeus, who had forbidden the gods and humans from **tampering** with the natural process of life and death. As a punishment Zeus killed Asclepius.

Myths as Memories

Many experts believe the story of Medusa and her sisters arose from a Greek civilization that had fallen long before the time of Hesiod. Modern scholars call that ancient era the **Bronze Age** because its people used tools and weapons made of the metal bronze. During the Bronze Age powerful kings ruled from magnificent palaces. For reasons that are still unclear, the Bronze Age civilization collapsed around 1200 B.C. For more than three centuries they lived in extreme poverty in scattered villages. During this dark age the Greeks told tales about the old days, which they came to see as a sort of golden age. They

The Italian sculptor Bernini created his Head of Medusa in 1630.

called it the Age of Heroes. Most of Greece's colorful myths were based on imperfect, often distorted memories of the Bronze Age civilization.

Some scholars believe that the story of Medusa's frightful image and her death at Perseus's hands recall an ancient struggle between Bronze Age men and women. These experts say that women had a great deal of influence during the Bronze Age. Queens and religious priestesses were as powerful as, or even more powerful than, kings. The priestesses held secret ceremonies that men were not allowed to attend. In these rituals the women wore masks with exaggerated features.

At some point during the Bronze Age, Greek men took control of the society and women lost their power. After the collapse of the Bronze Age culture, dim memories of the priestesses' masks became the scary faces of the Gorgons. The long and possibly violent struggle for power between men and women was reduced to the tale of the male hero Perseus slaying the strong female figure Medusa.

Other scholars have suggested different sources for the Gorgon myths. One theory suggests that the Greeks borrowed these myths from the cultures of North Africa.

Scholar Stephen R. Wilk has a different theory. He thinks the tales of the Gorgons were made up to explain patterns of stars in the night sky known as constellations. The Greeks spent a great deal of

Pictured is the star group, or constellation, of Perseus as it appears in the night sky.

This drawing shows the figure of Perseus holding Medusa's head outlined by the constellation's stars.

time studying the night sky, searching for recognizable shapes among the stars. Once the Greeks found a shape, they would make up a story to explain how the figure got in the sky. In the constellation known as Perseus, the Greeks saw the hero holding a sword in his right hand and Medusa's head in his left. According to Wilk, this constellation inspired the myth.

The true origins of the Gorgon myths will likely never be known, but their story continues to fascinate each new generation.

Chapter 2:

Perseus Finds and Kills Medusa

Many stories about Medusa and her sisters were told in ancient times. By far the most important and popular myth told how the hero Perseus tracked down and slew the snake-haired Gorgon. This tale became one of the most famous of all the Greek myths.

How Perseus Was Tricked

At first Perseus did not take seriously the idea of hunting down and slaying the Gorgons. For one thing their island was far away and hard to reach. More importantly, to fight these creatures one had to look at them. And gazing on Medusa or one of her sisters meant certain death.

16

Eventually, however, Perseus changed his mind and decided to find and slay Medusa. The story begins with Perseus's mother, Danae. She was the daughter of the king of Argos, in southern Greece. Not long after Perseus's birth, Danae was forced to

Holding her infant son, Perseus, Danae flees the city of Argos in this twentieth-century drawing.

flee her native city. She and the baby ended up on the island of Sérifos, about a hundred miles south of Athens. After Perseus had grown into young manhood, Danae met the local ruler, Polydectes. Polydectes was taken with her beauty and asked Danae to marry him. She did not love him and refused. Polydectes kept insisting that she change her mind—until Perseus stepped in. He told the ruler to leave his mother alone.

Extremely angry at both Danae and Perseus, Polydectes plotted revenge. Being a coward, he was afraid to challenge Perseus to a fight. So he tried to trick the young man into doing something dangerous. Knowing that Perseus owned no horses, Polydectes demanded that every man on the island provide him with the gift of a horse. As the king ex-

This German drawing is based on one of the many ancient sculptures of Medusa.

pected he would, Perseus offered to do some service for Polydectes in return. It was then that the **vengeful** king sprang his trap. He asked the young man to go out and find the Gorgon Medusa, kill her, and bring back her head.

SEEKING DIVINE HELP

Although he was brave, Perseus knew he would need help to find and kill Medusa. For one thing Perseus had no idea where to find the island of the Gorgons. And rumors said Medusa had skin so tough that ordinary swords would not penetrate it. There was also the problem of how to fight her without having to look directly at her.

Perseus dealt with these concerns one at a time. He began by asking others if they knew where Medusa lived. The young man asked a number of knowledgeable people. Among them were some priestesses who claimed to speak for the gods. But none were able to tell him where to find the Gorgons' island.

Disappointed, Perseus was trying to decide what to do next when he received help from an unexpected source. As Perseus rode his horse along a country road, he saw a handsome young man carrying a golden staff with little wings on it. The young man said he was Hermes, the swift-footed messenger god and protector of travelers. Hermes said he had come to solve two of Perseus's problems and to offer advice about the third. First the deity offered to guide Perseus to the Gorgons' island. Hermes also produced a

magnificent sword and offered it to Perseus. The god said this was the only sword in the world with a blade sharp enough to slice through Medusa's thick skin.

The Three Old Hags

Hermes then addressed the problem of how to get close enough to Medusa to use the sword. To accomplish this feat, the god said, the young man would need four special tools. One of these would allow him to avoid the Gorgon's gaze and keep from being turned to stone. To obtain this tool, said Hermes, Perseus needed only to look up. Perseus did so and saw the goddess Athena floating down from the sky. She was dressed in a splendid suit of armor and carried a spear and a shield made of highly polished bronze. After greeting Perseus, Athena handed him the weapons. The goddess told Perseus to be sure he carried the shield when he faced Medusa. Rather than looking directly at the monster, Athena instructed, Perseus should use the shield as a mirror and look only at Medusa's reflection. The Gorgon's reflected image was harmless.

Perseus thanked the goddess, and she wished him luck and departed. Hermes then told Perseus about the other three tools he would need to fight Medusa. These were guarded by the **Nymphs** of the North, beautiful maidens who lived in a secret place. The only beings in the world who knew the location were the Graiae. The three old hags who shared a single eye were the Gorgons' sisters, Hermes reminded Perseus,

In this illustration, Perseus holds the eye of the Graiae, who beg him to return it.

Perseus Finds and Kills Medusa

so they would probably refuse to help anyone who wanted to harm Medusa. Perseus would have to find a way to trick the Graiae into revealing the information.

At the Edge of the World

With Hermes' aid, Perseus located the cave of the Graiae in a remote, barren land near the edge of the known world. The young man saw three old women sitting in the dirt near the cave's entrance. He watched them for a while and observed their odd behavior. Each time one of them wanted to look at something, she took the eye out of her sister's fore-

An ancient sculpture depicts the god Hermes and three nymphs.

head and placed it in an empty socket in her own forehead. As Perseus looked on, the wrinkled, old sisters exchanged the eye every minute or so.

The sharing of the eye gave Perseus an idea. He boldly stepped forward and greeted the Graiae. One of the hags asked what he wanted, and Perseus answered that he was looking for the home of the Nymphs of the North. Hearing this, the weird sisters hissed at Perseus and ordered him to go away. But the young man had no intention of leaving without the information he needed. He suddenly jumped to one side of the Graiae. Panicked, one hag demanded the eye so she could see what the intruder was doing. Perseus then jumped to another sister and then back to the first. To keep track of him, the sisters had to pass the eye back and forth as quickly as possible. As they were exchanging the eye, Perseus reached out and grabbed it. The Graiae blinded, Perseus made his demand. Unless the sisters told him how to find the nymphs, he would not return their eye. The Graiae moaned and wailed, pleading with Perseus to change his mind, but he refused. Finally the hags gave in and told the young man where to find the nymphs.

The Three Gifts

The young man wasted no time in following the Graiae's directions. He headed north and after many days' journey reached the home of the secretive but friendly nymphs. The young maidens gave him the three remaining objects he needed to fight Medusa.

One was a pair of winged sandals that allowed their wearer to fly. Another was a special sack that grew smaller or larger as needed, depending on how big an object one placed in it. The third was a magical cap that made its wearer invisible. Combining these gifts with the special sword and shield provided by Hermes and Athena, Perseus felt ready to take on the snake-haired monster.

The Island of the Gorgons

With Hermes at his side pointing the way, Perseus flew over distant, uncharted lands and waterways. According to Ovid, Perseus and Hermes traveled "through thick-bearded forests, and tearing rocks and stones" until they came to the Gorgons' rocky island home. There Perseus beheld a weird and tragic sight. "As he looked about from left to right," Ovid wrote, "no matter where he turned, he saw both man and beast turned into stone, all creatures who had seen Medusa's face."[4]

Soon Perseus came upon the three Gorgons, who were sleeping on top of a large rock. He did not look at them directly. Following Athena's advice he viewed the reflection of the creatures in his shield. Suddenly Medusa awoke. She seemed to sense that danger was nearby. Thanks to the cap of invisibility, Perseus remained unseen.

For several moments Perseus floated above Medusa. Staring at the Gorgon in his glistening shield, Perseus watched the loathsome green snakes slither

A look of horror is frozen on the face of the slain Medusa in this seventeenth-century painting.

across her head. He shifted his eyes to Medusa's neck. His target sighted, Perseus swooped down on the monster. He raised his sword, and with one swift blow he sliced off Medusa's head. As the creature's body slumped to the ground, Perseus caught the **severed** head in his magic sack.

The sound of Medusa's body hitting the ground awoke Stheno and Euryale. Seeing their sister dead, the remaining Gorgons glanced around, hoping to catch the eyes of the culprit and turn him to stone. Perseus was still invisible, and he refused

Holding Medusa's head, Perseus soars in the sky on the flying horse Pegasus.

to look at the hideous sisters. The young man hurried away with his prize. As he flew over the graveyard of petrified corpses, Perseus took a last look back at Medusa's body. He watched in amazement as a winged horse arose from the blood of the slain Gorgon. In the birth of the magnificent creature known as Pegasus, ugliness and evil gave way to beauty and goodness.

Medusa

CHAPTER 3

MEDUSA COMES ALIVE

Rich with enchantment, danger, and heroism, the story of Medusa and Perseus has fascinated artists for more than two thousand years. Painters, sculptors, filmmakers, and now video-game creators have all kept the myth of the snake-haired Gorgon alive. Even today it inspires and entertains.

WORKS OF ART

Greek artists decorated vases with scenes of Perseus and Medusa as early as 700 B.C. Some vases depict the meeting of Athena and Perseus. Others show Medusa and her sisters. By far the most popular scene is the **beheading** of Medusa. The ancient Greeks believed the image of Medusa

27

American artist Alice Pike produced this version of
Medusa in 1892.

Medusa

could ward off evil and danger, so sculptors carved her likeness on front doors and walls of homes, on tombs, masks, and the shields of soldiers.

The Romans, who adopted many Greek gods and myths, portrayed the snake-haired Gorgon in **mosaics** and sculptures throughout their empire. One famous sculpture appears on a tomb in Florence, Italy. In the center of the sculpture is the head of Medusa. An image of Perseus is on one side and the goddess Athena on the other.

MEDUSA IN THE RENAISSANCE

Some of the world's greatest painters and sculptors have been challenged by the idea of depicting a face so horrible that just looking at it turned living beings to stone. Around 1500 the **Renaissance** master Leonardo da Vinci painted the severed head of Medusa lying face up. In the painting, detailed, lifelike snakes try to wriggle free of the Gorgon's head. About a hundred years later Michelangelo Merisi, known as Caravaggio, painted the head of the Gorgon as it fell to the ground, its eyes open, a look of shock on its face. Around 1610 the Flemish painter Peter Paul Rubens painted the head of Medusa lying on the ground, full of snakes writhing, fighting, and slithering away.

Perhaps the most famous work of art based on the story of Medusa is a sculpture by Florentine artist Benvenuto Cellini. Cellini was known as one of Europe's most skilled metalsmiths and sculptors.

Around 1540 Cellini's patron, the wealthy grand duke Cosimo de Medici, asked him to create a dramatic-looking statue. Cellini chose the slaying of Medusa as his subject. Completed in 1554, the huge bronze sculpture stands almost two stories high. It shows Perseus with his sword in his right hand at the end of his outstretched arm, and the severed head of Medusa dangling from his left hand.

Filmmakers Turn to Greek Mythology

The **advent** of motion pictures in the twentieth century meant that artists could bring the story of Medusa to life in a new way. Instead of being frozen on a canvas or in bronze or marble, the Gorgon and the serpents on her head could move. Creating a convincing Medusa proved a huge challenge, however.

The first Medusa in the movies was not played by a woman, but by a man. In *7 Faces of Dr. Lao*, Tony Randall plays the title character, a Chinese showman who brings his circus to a small town in the Old West. During the course of his show Dr. Lao changes into many different characters: Merlin the magician, the Greek god Pan, the abominable snowman, Apollonius of Tyana, a talking serpent, and Medusa. Watching the characters onstage, the residents of the small western town learn important lessons about themselves. To help Randall form the

Cellini's bronze masterpiece shows Perseus holding Medusa's severed head.

character of Medusa, makeup artist William J. Tuttle created a headdress of wriggling snakes. The film was a critical and box office success, and Tuttle later won two special Academy Awards for his work as a makeup artist.

The most amazing Medusa to appear in the movies was not played by a man or a woman. It was created by special-effects wizard Ray Harryhausen. After designing classic Greek monsters

Actor Tony Randall portrayed Medusa in the 1964 film 7 Faces of Dr. Lao.

such as Hydra and Cyclops for movies including *Jason and the Argonauts* and *The Seventh Voyage of Sinbad*, Harryhausen decided to bring more mythic beings to life. In the 1979 film *Clash of the Titans*, Harryhausen created several epic battles, including the confrontation between Perseus and Medusa.

In that scene Perseus finds Medusa inside a darkened room. The only light comes from the

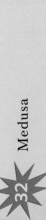

Medusa

glow of a fireplace. To make Medusa look more frightening, Harryhausen replaced her legs with a snakelike tail.

ANIMATING MEDUSA

Harryhausen's monsters, including Medusa, were not people in monster suits. Instead they were miniature models that Harryhausen made himself. To make the models appear to move, Harryhausen pre-pares to shoot an arrow at Perseus.

Ray Harryhausen's animated version of Medusa pre-pares to shoot an arrow at Perseus.

Perseus hides behind a pillar as he prepares to slay the monster.

built tiny metal skeletons with movable miniature joints called armatures. For Medusa, Harryhausen created separate armatures for the Gorgon's neck, shoulders, elbows, wrists, fingers, waist, and several more in the snakelike tail. Over the skeleton Harryhausen glued **latex** rubber molded to look like skin. He also added hair and scales. Finally he painted the model so that it looked very detailed and realistic.

Medusa

To make the Medusa model move, Harryhausen used a technique called stop-motion animation. The many armatures beneath the model's surface allowed him to move it into any position. First he placed the model in a realistic miniature version of the film set's darkened room. Then he set up his camera so that it was pointing directly at this table-top set. The camera was equipped with a button that snapped a single frame of film at a time. Under normal conditions a camera photographs twenty-four frames each second, and each frame is a tiny still photo. But when a projector shows that film at twenty-four frames a second, the images on the frames speed by, tricking the human eye with the illusion of motion.

CREATING AN ILLUSION

Harryhausen began by placing Medusa in a desired pose. Then he snapped one frame of film. Returning to the model Gorgon, he carefully moved some of its body parts a tiny bit. Then he took another frame of film. He repeated this process over and over again, slowly making the model Medusa go through all the motions called for in the scene. Later the thousands of frames Harryhausen had taken were projected at normal speed. This made Medusa appear to slither around the darkened room.

Medusa was not alone in the room, of course. Perseus was hunting her down with his sword and polished shield. Perseus was portrayed by the actor

Harry Hamlin. To create the illusion that the living actor and model Gorgon were the same size and in the same room, a camera crew shot **footage** of Hamlin moving around inside a full-size room. Harryhausen coached the actor beforehand, telling him all the moves he should make. Hamlin went through the motions of attacking Medusa while fighting nothing but thin air.

When Harryhausen shot the footage of Medusa, he projected the live-action footage of Hamlin onto a small screen built into his miniature set at the same time. Every time he snapped a frame of his tiny model, he also moved the film of Hamlin ahead one frame. The slow and painstaking process of matching live-action footage with miniature-action footage made it seem as if Hamlin's Perseus were fighting a full-size Medusa. The effect was stunning.

Marketing the Monster

Clash of the Titans was a box-office success and made Medusa part of popular culture. A number of companies obtained the rights to create toys and games based on the popular movie. In 1980 Mattel introduced a series of action figures based on *Clash of the Titans*. The Thermos company brought out a *Clash of the Titans* metal lunch box. It featured Perseus riding on Pegasus with his sword in one hand and the head of Medusa in the other. In 1981 the Whitman company released a *Clash of the Titans* board game that

Actor Harry Hamlin appears as Perseus in the 1979 movie Clash of the Titans.

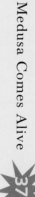

In this modern drawing, Medusa is a sea creature with seaweed hair.

retraced Perseus's adventures, including his battle with Medusa. The most unusual Medusa toy was introduced by Hasbro, makers of the clay product Play-Doh. The company's *Clash of the Titans* Medusa kit featured the Gorgon's head with holes through which the user could force the Play-Doh, creating a head full of snake hair.

Thanks to the success of *Clash of the Titans*, more companies created figurines based on the movie. In 1994, for example, the Geometric Design company introduced a finely detailed forty-piece model of Medusa in her lair.

Medusa has also found new life in card and computer games. Illustrator Darbury Stenderu designed a "Coils of the Medusa" card for the *Magic: the Gathering* collectible card game. This game allows players to compete against each other using an array of cards, each with its own strengths and weaknesses. Sony Computer Entertainment America introduced an action game for its PlayStation game system based on Disney's *Hercules* animated motion picture. The computer game features an encounter with Medusa in her lair. In 2002 Microsoft Game Studios released its epic *Age of Mythology* personal computer game that includes the character of Medusa. Players can use Medusa and other monsters against their enemies as they battle to control the universe.

Medusa has also been animated for television and motion pictures. The television series *Hercules* featured the voice of Jennifer Love Hewitt as Medusa. Pixar Animation Studio's 2001 animated movie *Monsters, Inc.* featured a purple-haired Medusa who works as a receptionist at the title company.

For twenty-five centuries, poets, painters, sculptors, and filmmakers have used their artistry to keep the story of the Gorgon alive. Through their efforts, the ghastly head with living snakes for hair continues to wash through the restless dreams and haunted imaginings of the human mind.

Medusa Comes Alive

NOTES

CHAPTER 1: ORIGINS OF THE HIDEOUS SISTERS

1. Aeschylus, *Aeschylus: The Suppliants, Seven Against Thebes, The Persians,* trans. Philip Vellacott. Baltimore: Penguin, 1961, p. 44.
2. Ovid, *Metamorphoses,* trans. Rolfe Humphries. Bloomington: University of Indiana Press, 1967, p. 135.
3. Hesiod, *Theogony,* in *Hesiod and Theognis,* trans. Dorothea Wender. New York: Penguin, 1973, p. 32.

CHAPTER 2: PERSEUS FINDS AND KILLS MEDUSA

4. Ovid, *Metamorphoses,* p. 134.

40

GLOSSARY

advent: Beginning.

beheading: The separation of the head from the body; decapitation.

Bronze Age: A period of human culture between the Stone Age and the Iron Age, characterized by the use of weapons and implements made of bronze.

footage: An amount of movie film, often measured in feet.

latex: A mixture of rubber or plastic in water used to make rubber products.

lethal: Able to kill; deadly.

mosaic: A picture made up of small colored pieces of stone or tile set into a surface.

nymph: A minor female deity inhabiting natural features such as trees, waters, and mountains.

Renaissance: The revival of classical art and learning that originated in Italy in the fourteenth century and later spread throughout Europe.

severed: Cut off.

tampering: Harmful interfering.

vengeful: Wanting to seek revenge.

For Further Exploration

Books

Philip Ardagh, *Ancient Greek Myths and Legends*. New York: Dillon, 1998. Beautifully illustrated by Virginia Gray, the book relates some of the most famous Greek myths and provides background about the tales.

David Bellingham, *An Introduction to Greek Mythology*. Secaucus, NJ: Chartwell, 1989. A basic introduction to the characters and events of Greek mythology.

Bernard Evslin, *Medusa*. New York: Chelsea House, 1987. A thorough retelling of the Medusa myth, from her undersea birth to her death at the hands of Perseus and eventual return to the sea.

Michael Gibson, *Gods, Men and Monsters from the Greek Myths*. New York: Peter Bedrick, 1977. Lavishly illustrated presentation of ancient Greek stories and myths.

Robert Graves, *Greek Gods and Heroes*. New York: Dell, 1960. The noted biographer offers a succinct version of the best-known Greek myths for young people.

Jen Green, *Myths of Ancient Greece*. Austin, TX: Steck-Vauhn, 2002. Illustrated with ancient and modern art, photographs, and maps, the book presents basic myths and provides background about the culture from which they emerged.

Warwick Hutton, *Perseus*. New York: Margaret K. McElderry, 1993. Hutton recounts and illustrates the episodes of Perseus's life, including his encounters with the Graiae and Medusa.

Deborah Nourse Lattimore, *Medusa*. New York: HarperCollins, 2000. Lushly illustrated by the author and set in large print, the book retells the Medusa story in condensed form.

Don Nardo, *Greek Mythology*. San Diego: KidHaven, 2002. Retells some of the classic ancient Greek myths for young readers.

Jeff Roven, *From the Land Beyond Beyond: The Films of Willis O'Brien and Ray Harryhausen*. New York: Berkley, 1977. A fascinating look at the films of the two greatest stop-motion animators of the twentieth century.

Stephanie Spinner, *Snake Hair: The Story of Medusa*. New York: Grosset and Dunlap, 1999. A colorfully illustrated version of the tale of the hideous sisters and Perseus's slaying of Medusa.

VIDEOS

Clash of the Titans, produced by Charles H. Schneer and Ray Harryhausen, directed by Desmond

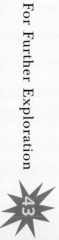

Davis. Burbank, CA: Warner Home Video, 2002. Combining live action and animation, the film depicts the adventures of Perseus.

7 Faces of Dr. Lao, produced and directed by George Pal. New York: MGM/UA Home Video, 1985. A Chinese showman arrives in the town of Abalone, Arizona, and enchants the townspeople with his magic circus.

The Storyteller: Perseus and the Gorgon, produced by Duncan Kenworthy, directed by David Garfath. Culver City, CA: Columbia TriStar Home Video, 1999. A live-action dramatization of the Greek myth with voice-over narration.

Web Sites

Amanda Kottke, "The Gorgons." (www.arthistory.sbc.edu/imageswomen/papers/kottkegorgon/gorgons.html.) An excellent site that discusses Medusa's and her sisters' backgrounds at length and also includes several ancient artistic renderings of Medusa.

"FortuneCity.com," "Clash of the Titans." (http://lavender.fortunecity.com/judidench/584/new-cott.html.) Part of a tribute to movie special-effects wizard Ray Harryhausen, this site features facts about, and sights and sounds from, the film in which Harryhausen animated the mythical monster Medusa.

Greek Mythology.com, "Medusa." (www.greek-mythology.com/Myths/Creatures/Medusa/medusa.html.) A brief but informative synopsis of the mythical character Medusa.

INDEX

PICTURE CREDITS

About the Author

Historian and award-winning author Don Nardo has written or edited many books about the ancient Greeks, including *Greek and Roman Sport, Life in Ancient Athens*, the *Greenhaven Encyclopedia of Greek and Roman Mythology*, and the four-volume *Library of Ancient Greece*. He lives with his wife Christine in Massachusetts.

A widely published poet and playwright, Bradley Steffens is the author and coauthor of twenty-five books for young adults, including *Loch Ness Monster* and *Cyclops*. He lives in Escondido, California, with his wife Angela and stepson John.